Getting dressed for WORK

STICKER ACTIVITY BOOK

Om KIDZ
An imprint of Om Books International

Nile wants to dress up as a doctor.
Can you help him?

Kate is a chef, all set to prepare delicious, yummy food. Help her get ready in her chef's clothes.

Sam wants to wear fireproof clothes and get dressed as a fire fighter. Choose the stickers and help him out.

Aaron wants to travel to the moon.
Dress him up as an astronaut.

It's time for work at the farm. Help Donny dress quickly by pasting the stickers.

Mac has so much to do! Help him dress as a traffic policeman to control the traffic.

What does Bob need to wear
to look like a soldier?

Pg-2
Pg-3
Pg-4
Pg-5

Pg-6

Pg-7

Pg-8

Pg-9

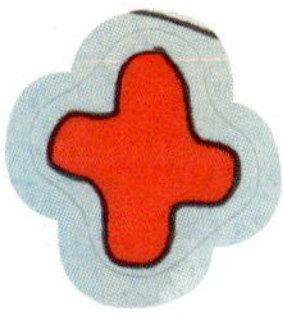
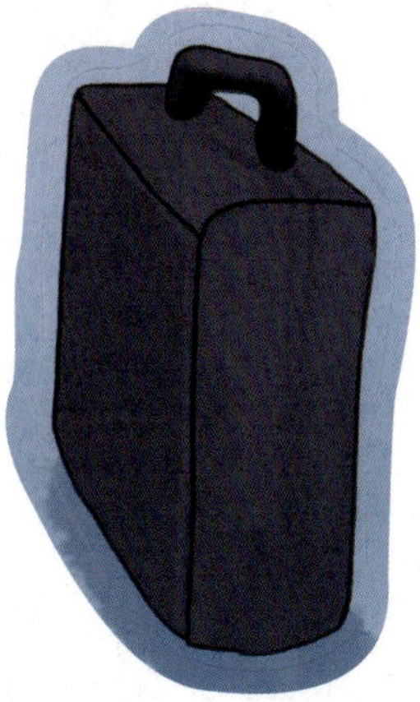

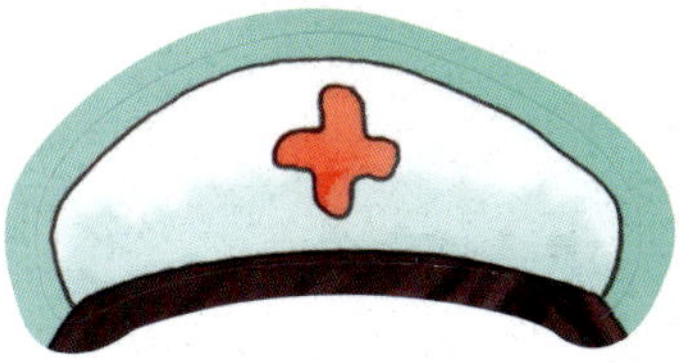

Pg-10

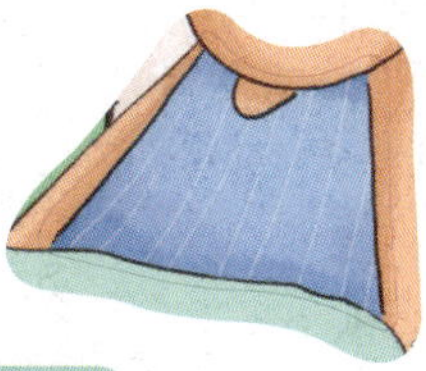

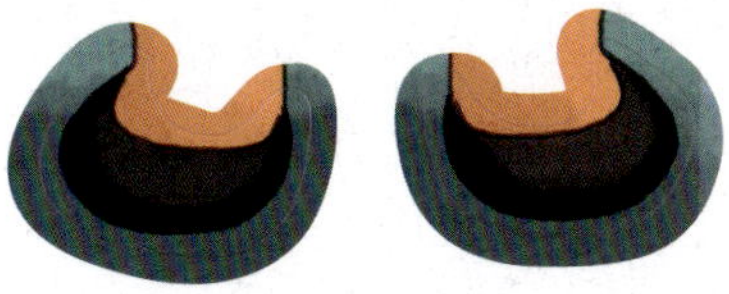
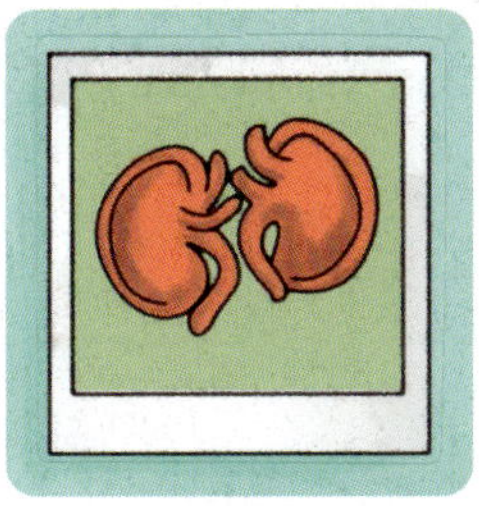

Pg-11

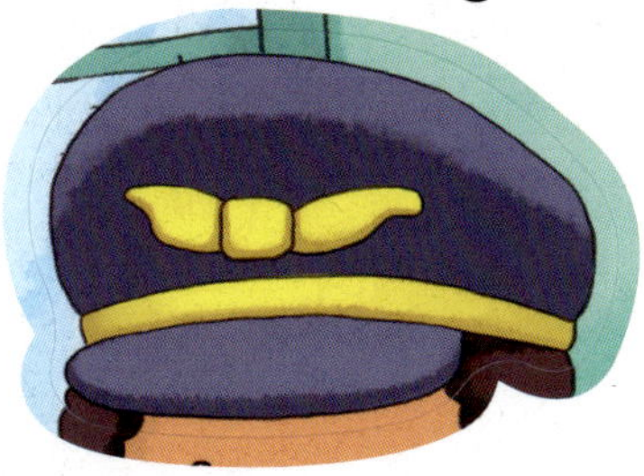

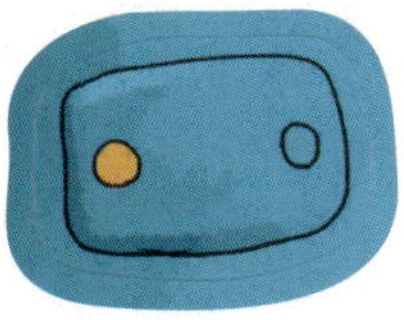

Pg-12

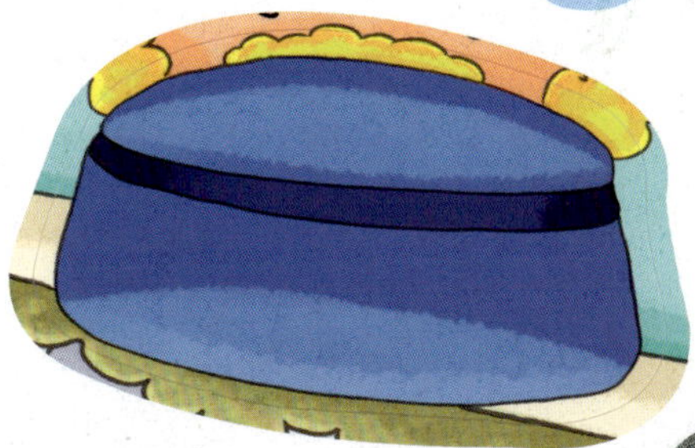
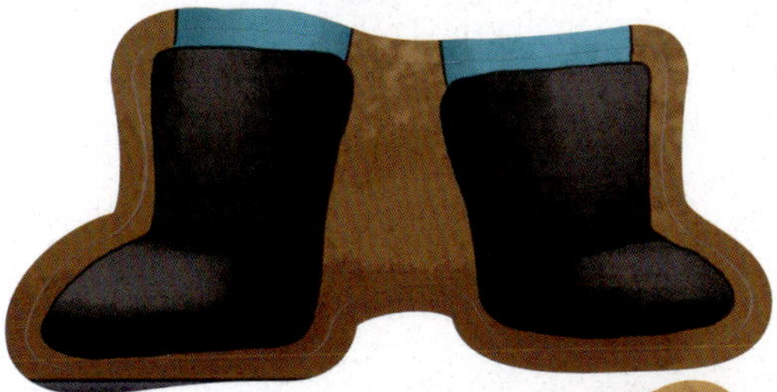

Pg-13

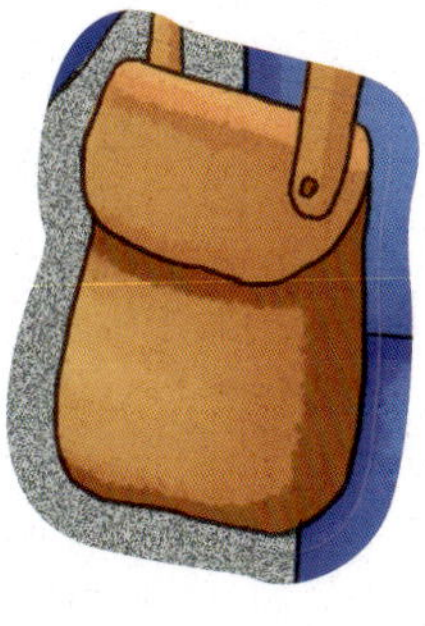
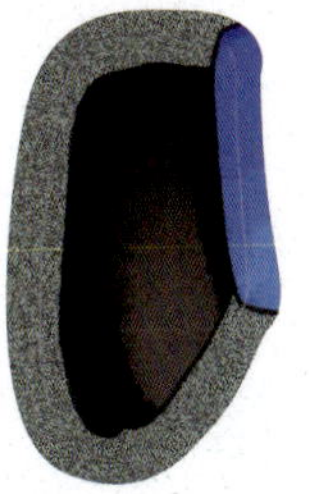

Pg-14

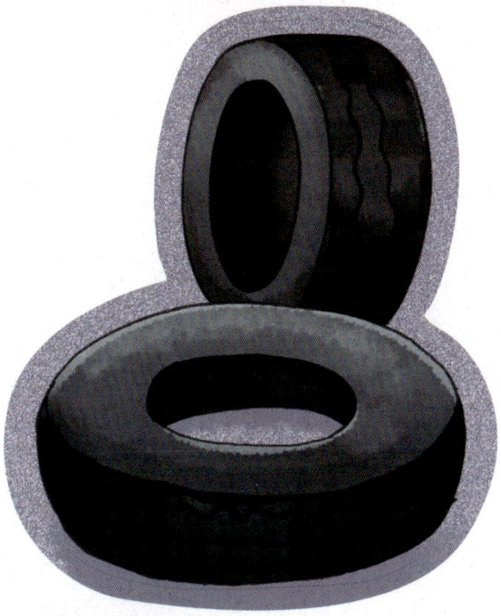

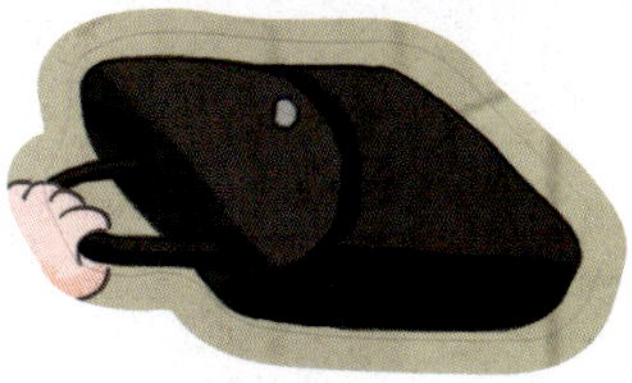

Pg-15

Pg-16

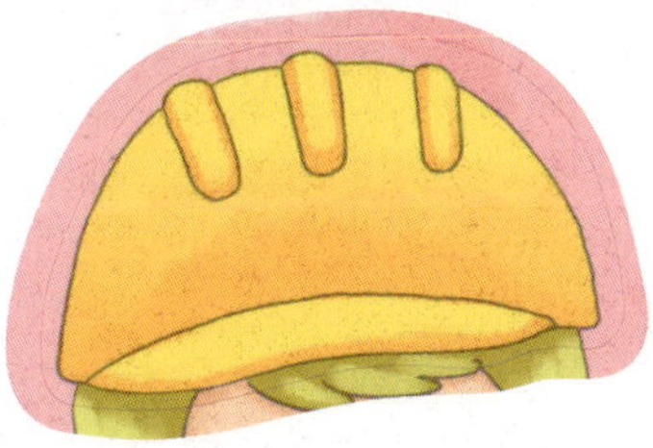

Ronny has to drive the school bus.
Use your stickers to dress him
up for the job.

Linda works at a hospital as a nurse.
Dress her up in the right clothes.

Finn wants to dress up as a pilot. Choose some clothes for him and help him get, set, go!

Jack is working hard in the mine with other miners. Pick out the stickers that complete the scene.

Hurry up! Help Jacob dress up as a postman. He has a lot of mails to deliver.

What does Andy need to dress up as a mechanic? Help him out.

Jill wants to dress up as a lawyer. Choose clothes for her and complete the picture.

Mia wants to dress up as an architect and draw up plans for a new building. Dress her up for the job!